Paul Lyndon Burtwell

Pray Like The Boss

1 THESS 5:17

Pray Like The Boss

Learn How To Pray The Jesus Way

By Paul Lyndon Burtwell, BAHons, PGCE, QTS

ISBN- 13

Published by ELIAS MEDIA

DEDICATION

To my Wife, Sarah Kathleen Burtwell
Whose support and encouragement made my ministry possible.

CONTENTS

PREFACE

Prayer is as vital today as it ever has been. It is the foundation of the Christian Spiritual life and the main source of strength in the life of a believer. Prayer is powerful and prayer works. In almost thirty years of ministry I have personally witnessed many incredible answers to pray and with each answer comes a tremendous surge of increased faith. Prayer begets faith and faith begets more prayer. Through prayer I have witnessed enemies toppled, spiritual forces driven out, wonderful healings and an 'almost' resurrection from the dead. Prayer has radically changed my life for the better along with millions of others who could testify to the same blessings. As prayer is so important in our lives, I thought it best to write a book about our Master or Boss, Jesus. After all, who could claim to know more about prayer than Jesus? Jesus was, is and forever will be the perfect example of how a human being should relate to God. So in this book I have made every effort to portray

Jesus in his correct historical light and setting. I have endeavoured to get to the heart of the Saviour regarding how he would want us to pray today, and in so doing I hope to unlock a world that many believers up until now, have been unaware of. So now may our wise Rabbi and Saviour bless you as you read these pages and learn How To Pray Like The Boss.

CHAPTER ONE
Why Pray Like The Boss?

Allow me to say this up front, Jesus is the eternal divine Son of God. He was and is the perfect human being. Fully God, fully man. If anyone in the history of the human race knew how to pray, it was Jesus. Prior to his incarnation here on earth, Jesus had spent uninterrupted fellowship with his father from eternity. This qualifies him as being the greatest teacher to humanity of how we should relate and converse with God. When we study the Scriptures we see Jesus praying regularly to his father in Heaven. Here are five clear examples,

"After he had dismissed them, he went up on a mountainside by himself to pray. Later that night, he was there alone,"

Matthew 14:23

"Very early in the morning, while it was still dark, Jesus got up, left the house and went off to a solitary place, where he prayed."

Mark 1:35

"One of those days Jesus went out to a mountainside to pray, and spent the night praying to God."

Luke 6:12

"About eight days after Jesus said this, he took Peter, John and James with him and went up onto a mountain to pray."

Luke 9:28

"One day Jesus was praying in a certain place. When he finished, one of his disciples said to him, 'Lord, teach us to pray, just as John taught his disciples."

Luke 11:1

Jesus considered prayer to be of the utmost importance. He lived prayer, he breathed prayer. To Jesus prayer was his intimate time with his father, enjoying that uninterrupted fellowship he once had. For those of us who do pray, we can confirm that time spent in prayer re-energises and rejuvenates us. There is something incredibly special about prayer that we often cannot quite describe. For myself when I pray, I feel as though I am plugged into the ultimate reality. Sometimes it feels as if this world is not real at all and that the ultimate reality is still waiting for us. And when I feel plugged into this ultimate reality, the worries, cares and stresses of this life seem to fall away and evaporate as in the words of the old song, 'the things of earth grow strangely dim.'

What is Prayer?

So what exactly is prayer? Put simply, prayer is connecting with God. Prayer can be spoken audibly, or shared quietly from the heart. It is not so much about the posture of the body, but rather the posture of the heart. It is about coming before God with a humble heart and truly recognising who you are in comparison to who he is. Spending a little time in meditation before you pray is also helpful in this manner. Sitting quietly and trying to imagine just how powerful, great and vast God is helps to attune our focus and awareness of him. Jewish people often call him 'The King of the Universe' in prayer and I think this is a worthy title for God. For who in this universe or any other is greater or more majestic than him?

The fact that such a great being cares about us should stagger our minds. As the psalmist writes,

"Lord, our Lord, how majestic is your name in all the earth! You have set your glory in the heavens. Through the praise of children and infants you have established a stronghold against your enemies, to silence the foe and the avenger. When I consider your

heavens, the work of your fingers, the moon and the stars, which you have set in place, what is mankind that you are mindful of them, human beings that you care for them?"

Psalm 8:1-4

God really does care about us. He really is concerned about every aspect of our lives. Only a quick perusal of the lives of people like Joseph or David in the Bible show how intricately God is working in our lives. And often during the difficult times, when it feels as though God is a million miles away, it is at this precise time that God is birthing a new chapter in our lives. When we think of Joseph, it wasn't until he was rejected by his family, sold as a slave and then falsely accused by Potiphar's wife, that he began to mature into the future Prime Minister of Egypt that God had called him to be.

When we think of David, it was not until he was overlooked by his family, mocked by Goliath and almost pinned to a wall with a spear that he matured into the King of Israel that he was called to be. With God on our side difficult times do not destroy us, they define us. As someone rightly said, 'We are in training for reigning.' And because of this we can be certain that God is with us in the good times and in the bad, in the high times and in the low. He is with us because he cares for us. As the Apostle Paul encourages,

"And we know that in all things God works for the good of those who love him, who have been called according to his purpose."
Romans 8:28

Right now, this very second, God is working all things together for your good. You may not realise it, and you almost certainly cannot see it, but when the breakthrough comes, you will look back and see his handiwork. God is so intimately involved in our lives and this should give us a confidence in prayer that otherwise would not be validated. For if God knows us inside out so to speak, then there is nothing we need to try and hide from him. He sees all and knows all. He is the one person that we can be totally honest and totally open with, without the fear of judgement and condemnation. Yes, he may correct us, for who among us can say we do not need correction! But this correction is for our good, to help us and to bless us. To make us more like God so we can have a more intimate relationship with him.

Does Prayer Work?

But does prayer work? Well, that depends on what someone means by work. If they mean that they will get whatever they want, whenever they want, as if God were some big blue genie who will give them unlimited wishes, then no. However, if they mean will God listen to me, will God change me and will God consider my requests, then yes, prayer does indeed work. I can personally testify to the fact that I have felt God's presence in prayer, that he has changed me for the better through prayer and that he has considered my requests, and on many occasions has granted me those requests. As amazing as this aspect is, namely that God will listen to our requests and answer, we must be enormously careful not to think of God as some great big vending machine (i.e. put a prayer in and get a prize out). God is not a genie, he is not a vending machine and he is certainly not the wonderful Wizard of Oz. God is a great King, God is the Creator of all things and God is our father. Therefore, we must show him the honour and respect he is due, just as Jesus did when he walked the earth.

The foundation of all prayer should be love. God's love for us and our love for God. Prayer is not some cold, formal religious thing. It is a vibrant, heartfelt and emotional experience. Prayer should come from an honest heart with all the drama that entails. Some prayers will be full of joy whilst others may be full of sorrow. Some prayers will be loud and full of hutzpah whilst others may be quiet and sombre. Prayer should not be prescribed, but alive with the heartbeat of the person praying. But is not this type of prayer irreverent? Not at all, in fact when we study the prayers of the Scriptures this is how the Hebrews often prayed. Take this example from Jesus' own life,

"During the days of Jesus' life on earth, he offered up prayers and petitions with fervent cries and tears to the one who could save him from death, and he was heard because of his reverent submission."
Hebrews 5:7

Also, the Lord's brother the Apostle James encourages us to pray with passion when he writes,

"Confess your faults one to another, and pray one for another, that you may be healed. The effectual fervent prayer of a righteous man avails much."
James 5:16

The Greek word used here for ‘effectual fervent’ is ‘energeo’ and it means to pray with some energy, effort and strength. When we love God with all of our heart, and his desires become our desires, then we will feel impassioned and burdened to pray his will into being. There will be no stopping it, and as strange and alarming as this may sound, it really is not an unpleasant thing. For the life and energies of God sustain you and encourage you in prayer. It is in fact quite a wonderful thing, a supernatural thing, and a privilege that very few people ever truly encounter.

Wonders Through Prayer

Some years ago I was holidaying in Dorset on the English coast, when I received a telephone call from my sister advising me to return home. In the telephone call my sister had told me that my mother had contracted the pneumococcal virus and had been taken into hospital. Upon hearing this we returned home and visited my mother in hospital who was finding it increasingly difficult to breath. After placing her on the antibiotics and medicine available, and observing that none of it was working, they moved my mother to the Intensive Care Unit. As she grew progressively worse, they performed a tracheotomy on her (this is a procedure where they cut an opening in the throat to insert a breathing tube into a patients lungs). As her health continued to decline, the doctors advised there was nothing more they could do for my mother and they asked us to call the family to come in to say their goodbyes. By this stage, my mother was not conscious and her lungs were now struggling to push out the carbon dioxide gas. In essence she was slowly suffocating, and the doctors suggested turning off the life-support machine and allowing her to die peacefully.

My family was devastated, we had only just been enjoying ourselves on holiday and now we were faced with this. I had never lost a parent so I really didn't know how to respond, my whole body felt numb and lost. I can remember retiring to the closest toilet, locking the door, holding my hands in the air and thanking God, for giving me such a wonderful mother. I praised him for the massive influence she had been on my life and I worshipped him. After spending a few moments in prayer, I returned to my family in the room with my mother. My sister was there, who is also a follower of Jesus, and we talked about praying the prayer of faith that we read about in the book of James, Chapter 5. So together, we agreed to lay hands upon her and to pray, asking God to heal her. As we began to pray I sensed the presence of a huge angel at the head of my mother's bed. I did not see an angel, when I looked there was nobody there. But I could somehow feel him, or sense him, as if out of the corner of my eye he was standing there looking down at her. Encouraged by this feeling I continued to pray. As we continued in prayer throughout the evening, my mother's carbon dioxide levels began to drop and her oxygen levels began to increase. We were watching a miracle unfold right before our eyes. God was healing my mother. And as remarkable as this may sound, within five days she was home and much improved.

During my time in ministry I have witnessed many such remarkable answers to prayer. Answers that have stunned me and have revealed to me that my faith had not been quite enough, yet God did it anyway. To repeat what I said earlier, this is not to say that every time we pray for someone to be healed they will be, or that every time we pray for a job we will get it. But it is to say that God hears, and God answers, his way and in his time and he does this because he cares for you.

"Cast all your anxiety on him because he cares for you."
1 Peter 5:7

And so we pray like the Boss, Jesus, because Jesus and Jesus alone is the perfect example of how we as servants and children of God should pray.

CHAPTER TWO
The Context Of The Boss

If I have not heard it a hundred times then I have not heard it at all, "Context is King!" This maxim, or rule applies to all Scriptural interpretation. Context is the canvas upon which theological ideas and understanding must be painted. One reason why different groups within the Christian tradition differ on theological interpretations is due in part to a lack of contextual understanding. Let me give you an illustration.

Martin's Misunderstanding

Martin is a business man who works in the city of London. He has an important business appointment in China coming up, however he cannot speak a word of Chinese. So downloading an 'English to Chinese' app on his phone, Martin heads off to Beijing. At first, Martin seems to be able to conduct his way around Beijing without too much difficulty but then the heavens open and the rain comes down in sheets. Having nothing but a briefcase, he holds it above his head as a makeshift umbrella and finally arrives at his destination, a towering office block in the heart of the city. Upon arrival, he is warmly welcomed into the business centre and sits down to await the important meeting. Only moments after Martin sits down a team of about ten business executives file into the meeting room and greet Martin with the words, "Nǐ hǎo." Martin quickly holds his phone up to their lips to catch this phrase and the phone translates, "Hello." One of the executives continues to speak, "Nǐ de lǚchéng zěnme yàng?" Martin quickly shoves the phone under his lips and it translates, "How was your journey?" Martin is more than chuffed with himself that he had the ingenuity to purchase the correct app and now it is Martin's turn to respond. Holding the phone up to his lips in a rather triumphant manner he responds, "Not great. The heavens opened on me!"

As the Beijing executives listen to the interpretation their eyes become wide and one of them runs to the window yelling, "Tiānkōng zài fēnliè!" He then darts out of the room. A little bit taken aback, Martin continues, "Yes, and it was coming down like sheets." The phone app continues to translate. "Chuángdān!" cries another executive as he too runs to the window and then darts out of the meeting room. "Yes…" Martin continues hesitantly. "It's raining cats and dogs out there." At which point all of the executives scream and run out of the office.

Healthy Eyes And Unhealthy Eyes?

This illustration, hopefully, will make you realise that translation without context can lead to some disastrous results. Now, coming back to Jesus and to prayer, our English translations of the Holy Bible are some of the best translations in the world. In the United Kingdom, we have some of the finest Greek and Hebrew Scholars. In fact my former Professor,

Gordon Wenham, helped to oversee many of the translations we are privileged to have with us today. However, we must also understand the limitations of each translation. If we think back to the illustration, the idioms of, 'the heavens opened', 'coming down like sheets' and 'it is raining cats and dogs', are perfectly acceptable English idioms, in the United Kingdom. But take these phrases outside of the United Kingdom and you might get some funny looks, you may even see some executives running for cover. This is because these idioms are contextual. They belong somewhere, namely the United Kingdom. So this is where we need to put our thinking caps on, because the English translations of the Holy Bible are good, but they do not convey Hebrew idioms and popular phrases too well. As Jesus was a Hebrew speaking, Jewish Rabbi, who lived in first century Israel, we need to understand these. Let us also not forget that the English language was not even in existence in his day.

Let me give you an example of what I mean, taken from the teaching of Jesus himself,

"Do not store up for yourselves treasures on earth, where moths and vermin destroy, and where thieves break in and steal. But store up for yourselves treasures in heaven, where moths and vermin do not destroy, and where thieves do not break in and steal. For where your treasure is, there your heart will be also.

'The eye is the lamp of the body. If your eyes are healthy, your whole body will be full of light. But if your eyes are unhealthy, your whole body will be full of darkness. If then the light within you is darkness, how great is that darkness!

'No one can serve two masters. Either you will hate the one and love the other, or you will be devoted to the one and despise the other. You cannot serve both God and Money."

Matthew 6:19-24

At first reading, the first and last paragraph of this teaching seems to makes sense. Jesus is instructing us not to store up treasures on earth and to serve only God and not money and that is pretty straight forward. But what about that middle paragraph that speaks of healthy and unhealthy eyes? What on earth could this mean? I have heard some Ministers interpret these words as a warning to be careful as to what you watch on television. Other Ministers have taught on these verses referencing the curse of spiritual blindness and the blessing of spiritual revelation, so thus, different Ministers come to different conclusions, because the context is not clearly understood.

So what is the context here? Let us have a look at a few of them:

1. The Geographical context is Israel
2. The Historical context is the first century
3. The Cultural context is a Jewish one subjugated by Rome
4. The Linguistic context is Hebrew/Aramaic

5. The Author context is the Jewish Rabbi Jesus (Yeshua)
6. The Receiver context is the Jewish disciples of Jesus
7. The Translation context is English translated from Greek, having been translated from Hebrew/ Aramaic
8. The Textual context appears to be Jesus teaching about wealth

Let's Put This All Together

With this in mind, we now need to retrofit this second paragraph (which we read in English), back into its original contextual form, but how do we do this?

Well, firstly we need to see what the original Greek actually says.

If we study the words for 'eyes are healthy' and look at the Greek we see this phrase, "ὀφθαλμός ὦ ἁπλοῦς", which means "Single Eye".

Next, if we take the words 'eyes are unhealthy' and look at the Greek we see this phrase, "ὀφθαλμός ὦ πονηρός", meaning "Bad Eye".

By discovering this we are now one step closer to what Jesus actually said. Now we need to take a look at early Jewish literature to see if anything 'pops' out at us that fulfils the above contextual parameters. Let us take a look at the Jewish teaching from around the time of Jesus and for this we need to look into the Mishnah (also known as 'The Tradition of the Elders' or 'The Oral Law'),

"Whoever possesses these three things, he is of the disciples of Abraham, our father; and [whoever possesses] three other things, he is of the disciples of Balaam, the wicked. A good eye, a humble spirit and a moderate appetite he is of the disciples of Abraham, our father. An evil eye, a haughty spirit and a limitless appetite he is of the disciples of Balaam, the wicked. What is the difference between the disciples of Abraham, our father, and the disciples of Balaam,

the wicked? The disciples of Abraham, our father, enjoy this world, and inherit the world to come, as it is said: "I will endow those who love me with substance, I will fill their treasuries" (Proverbs 8:21). But the disciples of Balaam, the wicked, inherit gehinnom, and descend into the nethermost pit, as it is said: "For you, O God, will bring them down to the nethermost pit those murderous and treacherous men; they shall not live out half their days; but I trust in You" (Psalms 55:24)."

Mishnah Pirkei Avot 5:19

And so, we immediately find in the Mishnah the Hebrew idioms of 'Ayin Ha-Tovah' and the 'Ayin Ha-Ra' or the 'Good Eye' and the 'Bad Eye'.

Now the 'Good Eye' was a person who was considered loving and generous, whereas the 'Evil Eye' was a person who was considered unloving and stingy. When we feed this information back into the teaching of Jesus it makes much more sense. Here is my attempt at doing just this,

"Do not store up for yourselves treasures on earth, where moths and vermin destroy, and where thieves break in and steal. But store up for yourselves treasures in heaven, where moths and vermin do not destroy, and where thieves do not break in and steal. For where your treasure is, there your heart will be also.
The eye is the lamp of the body. If you are a loving and generous person, your whole body will be full of light (goodness and righteousness). But if you are an unloving and stingy person, your whole body will be full of darkness (wickedness and sin). If then the light within you is darkness, how great is that darkness!
'No one can serve two masters. Either you will hate the one and love the other, or you will be devoted to the one and despise the other. You cannot serve both God and Money."
Matthew 6:19-24

Does not this reading make a lot more sense? Especially within the context of treasures, wealth and the love of money and so this is why we should always strive to understand the context, as well as the translation. Once we understand the context, then the lid is flipped off of the treasure chest of God's word and we begin to make sense of many of the difficult sayings and apparent contradictions that appear in the English translations. As the purpose of this book is to teach you how to pray like our Boss, Jesus, this is what we are going to need to do. Why? Well, a lot of what Jesus has to say about prayer is deeply rooted in Jewish tradition. Many of the phrases and idioms that Jesus used have multilayered meanings and this understanding immediately transforms our study from a monotone lesson, to an exciting multihued adventure of discovery.

X Marks The Spot!

If you are anything like me, you love the great adventure films. The fights, the explosions, the action! One of my favourite series in this genre are the Indiana Jones movies, with Harrison Ford leading as the titular character. There is a great scene in the third instalment where Indy holds only half of the instructions that his father left him in a diary, instructions that lead to the famed Holy Grail. Indy must travel to Venice to find the other half of the instructions, and after smashing through a library floor ("X marks the spot!"), breaking down a wall and wading through rat infested petroleum, he finally arrives at the tomb of Sir Richard. After pushing back the lid on the sarcophagus, he discovers the Knight holding a sword and shield. Right there on the shield is an engraving which contains the second part of instructions that Indy needs to fulfil his quest. It is a great moment in the film and we know as the audience that from this point on, the film is going to get really interesting.

Now, by understanding the importance of 'Translation plus Context', we also have received the two parts of our instructions to continue on our great quest, to discover how to pray like the Boss. For if we only had the translation and not the context of Jesus' first century life, our journey into prayer may have been halted and even stopped. The reason for this, is because before we can understand the way Jesus prayed, we must first understand the vital importance and centrality of the Jewish 'Amidah'.

CHAPTER THREE
The Amidah Of The Boss

A poor young Jewish boy named Eli, was walking through a forest wondering where his next meal would come from. As he strolled along, out of the corner of his eye a bright flickering glow caught his attention. Being well versed in the doctrines and the traditions of the elders, he immediately recognised it as the Shekinah of God. Taking off his well worn shoes and bowing his face to the ground, this young Jew began to pray,

"Blessed art Thou, O Lord our God, King of the universe…"

All of a sudden, Eli is interrupted by a voice emanating from the glowing flames,

"What can I do for you young man?"

A little taken aback, Eli responds, "Lord, will you permit me to ask you a few questions?"

"Of course." replied the voice, "What would you like to know."

Becoming a little braver Eli asks, "Lord what is a thousand years like to you?"

The voice responds, "A thousand years is as a second to me, and a second is as a thousand years."

"Hmmm." Pondered Eli. "And Lord what is a thousand dollars like to you?"

The voice responds, "A thousand dollars is as a penny to me, and a penny is as a thousand dollars."

Straightening up Eli asks, "Lord, you know all things and you know I'm a poor boy. Please can I have a thousand dollars?"

"Sure!" replied the voice, "Just wait one second!"

Prayer is part and parcel of everyday Jewish life and as Jesus was a Jewish Rabbi living in first century Israel, he would have been very familiar with the Jewish prayer called, The Amidah. The Amidah is considered the most important prayer within Judaism and it is the core practice during the four times of prayer known as shacharit (morning prayer), mincha (afternoon prayer), maariv (evening prayer) and mussaf (further prayer). The fact that the Amidah is to be prayed everyday is taught by the esteemed Rabban Gamaliel,

"One must say the Eighteen everyday."
m. Berachot 4:3

The Amidah also known as HaShemoneh Esreh (The Eighteen) was originally composed of eighteen sections known as the eighteen blessings and is called the Amidah (standing), because when it is recited it is done so in the standing position.

While reciting the Amidah, it is important for the person to focus on the meaning of the words being uttered and to remind themselves that they are standing in the holy presence of God. Also, just prior to reciting the Amidah the practitioner is to take three steps backwards and then three steps forwards, as if one were approaching a King. In traditional Judaism the prayer is to be recited quietly, so that others cannot hear your words (however more volume is permitted when alone), and always with your feet together.

To give you a flavour of the Amidah, here is an extract from the sixth section for the forgiveness of sin,

"Forgive us, O our Father, for we have sinned;
pardon us, O our King, for we have transgressed; for you pardon and forgive.
Blessed are you, O Lord, who is merciful and always ready to forgive."

The Amidah Prayer, The Sixth Blessing

And here is a further extract asking for the exaltation of the Messianic King,

"Speedily cause the offspring of your servant David to flourish,
and let him be exalted by your saving power,

for we wait all day long for your salvation.
Blessed are you, O Lord, who causes salvation to flourish."

The Amidah Prayer, The Fifteenth Blessing

What is really interesting about the Amidah prayer, is that although it can be recited in about five minutes, in times of distress and emergency, Rabbi's would often provide their disciples with a condensed or shortened version of the prayer to perform.

Here are a couple of extracts from these condensed Amidah's and I would like you to notice if there is anything familiar about them,

"May your will be done in heaven above, grant peace of mind to those who fear you [on earth] below, and do what seems best to you. Blessed are you, O LORD, who answers prayer."

Rabbi Eliezar

Other sages say: "The needs of your people Israel are many but they do not know how to ask for their needs. May it be your will, O Lord our God, to sustain each and every one and to supply each person what is needed. Blessed are you, O Lord, who answered prayer."

The Babylonian Talmud Berachot 29b

The Lord's Prayer

Sometimes when we read the New Testament Gospels, there are some phrases that do not appear to make an awful lot of sense to the English reader. As we revealed in the last chapter with the Good Eye and the Bad Eye example. There are of course many others that could be mentioned, but one of interest, that seems to stand out like a sore thumb is found in the Gospel of Luke,

"One day Jesus was praying in a certain place. When he finished, one of his disciples said to him, "Lord, teach us to pray, just as John taught his disciples."

Luke 11:1

At first blush one could ask, 'What is so strange about this request?' But this is to underestimate the religious life of the first century Jew, living in Israel. Just think about it. How could these men not know how to pray? They were Jews, raised in the synagogue, steeped in religious traditions. By the age of thirteen, in preparation for their bar mitzvah they would have been required to know and understand the Torah (the five books of Moses) and the Mishnah (the oral traditions),

"He used to say "At five years old [one is fit] for the Scripture, at ten years for the Mishnah, at 13 for the [the fulfilling of] commandments, at fifteen for the

Talmud, at eighteen for the bride-chamber, at twenty for pursuing [a calling]..."
The Mishnah, Pirkei Avot 5:21

Any Jewish man worth his salt, would have known the Amidah prayer verbatim (and let us not overlook the fact that at least two of them had already been disciples of John the Baptist, cf. John 1:35-40). In addition to this, one would naturally assume that the disciples would have heard their own Rabbi praying and even on occasion have been included in a time of prayer together. It seems like a very peculiar request when we view it in context... unless, they were asking for something a little deeper.

You Have Heard That It Was Said

The Sermon on the Mount is one of the clearest examples of Jesus correcting faulty Pharisaic theology. The purpose of Jesus producing the Sermon on the Mount was to reveal to the people of Israel the

Messiah's interpretation of the Mosaic Law as compared and contrasted with the Pharisaic interpretation of that same Law. In the Sermon, Jesus corrects many of the ideas of the Pharisees and restores to Israel the proper understanding of what God, through Moses was trying to convey. Namely that God expects obedience to his Law both externally 'and internally' as Jesus' teaching on adultery clearly shows. From a Pharisaic perspective you were only guilty in God's sight of committing adultery if you carried out the physical act. However, Jesus corrected this faulty view with these words,

"You have heard that it was said, "You shall not commit adultery." But I tell you that anyone who looks at a woman lustfully has already committed adultery with her in his heart. If your right eye causes you to stumble, gouge it out and throw it away. It is better for you to lose one part of your body than for your whole body to be thrown into hell. And if your right hand causes you to stumble, cut it off and throw

it away. It is better for you to lose one part of your body than for your whole body to go into hell."
Jesus, Matthew Chapter 5:27-30

So now, in a similar fashion, Jesus is asked by his disciples to teach them his condensed interpretation of the Amidah, also known as HaTefillah (The Prayer). And with the Messiah's interpretation of HaTefillah, Jesus will affirm that which is correct, correct that which is wrong and add his own personal theological insight.

The most complete response of Jesus' interpretation can be found in the Gospel of Matthew,

"This, then, is how you should pray:
Our Father in heaven, hallowed be your name.
Your kingdom come, your will be done, on earth as it is in heaven.
Give us today our daily bread.

And forgive us our debts, as we also have forgiven our debtors.
And lead us not into temptation.
But deliver us from the evil one.
For yours is the kingdom and the power and the glory forever. Amen."
Jesus, Matthew Chapter 6:9-13

As we can see from this Scripture, Jesus condensed the eighteen blessings of the Amidah to seven concise prayer points. Easy enough for the disciples to memorise, profound enough to stimulate their deeper thoughts.

Why Here Why Now?

Messianic expectation was high in the first century. The Prophet Daniel had given the Jewish people a timetable for the appearance of the Messiah and now, according to their reckoning, the countdown to the coming of the Messiah had been fulfilled. So where was he? All that had appeared was this Galilean peasant from Nazareth. Hardly the place for the glorious Messiah to hail from. Yet, Jesus continued to baffle the authorities by doing those things which only the Messiah, in his Kingdom age, should be able to do. A clear understanding of early Messianic expectation can be found in a partially fragmented work entitled, 'The Messianic Apocalypse', which was discovered in the Dead Sea Scrolls,

"[the hea]vens and the earth will listen to His Messiah ["anointed one"], and none therein will stray from the commandments of the holy ones.
Seekers of the Lord, strengthen yourselves in His service!
All you hopeful in (your) heart, will you not find the Lord in this?
For the Lord will consider the pious (hasidim) and call the righteous by name.
Over the poor His spirit will hover and will renew the faithful with His power.

And He will glorify the pious on the throne of the eternal Kingdom.
He who liberates the captives, restores sight to the blind, straightens the b[ent]
And f[or] ever I will cleav[ve to the h]opeful and in His mercy...
And the fr[uit...] will not be delayed for anyone.
And the Lord will accomplish glorious things which have never been as [He...]
For He will heal the wounded, and revive the dead and bring good news to the poor
...He will lead the uprooted and knowledge...and smoke."

The Messianic Apocalypse, Dead Sea Scroll 4Q521

As we can clearly see from these verses, the Messianic figure was expected to do several things: liberate the captives, restore sight to the blind, straighten the bent, heal the wounded, revive the dead and bring good news to the poor.

And this is exactly what Jesus did. In fact, Jesus was so well known as a miracle worker that the first century historian, Josephus, mentions Jesus and his 'wonderful works'. But for the Pharisees and Sadducees there was a major problem. How could this miracle worker from Nazareth be the Messiah, when he repeatedly humiliated them, challenged their theology and insisted on breaking the traditions of the elders? Now, either they were wrong, or Jesus was wrong. Guess which option they chose?

And so, in the second largest mistake of human history (Eve's rebellion being the first), the Jewish leadership opted to reject Jesus' claim of Messiahship on the grounds of demonic possession (cf. Matthew 12). Yes, the leadership of Israel agreed with one voice that Jesus was performing the miracles of the Messiah. But, only because he was himself possessed by Beelzebub, the chief of demons. With this official rejection of the Messiahship of Jesus, the offer of the Kingdom of God was rescinded and from that day forward, Jesus would only speak in parables and perform secret miracles. In fact, only one more miracle was promised to the Jewish nation and that was the sign of the Prophet Jonah, the sign of coming resurrection. It is in the shadow of this distress and emergency that the Lord's Prayer was born.

CHAPTER FOUR
The Father Of The Boss

"This, then, is how you should pray: Our Father in heaven, hallowed be your name."
Jesus, Matthew Chapter 6:9

"Judah ben Tema said: Be strong as a leopard, and swift as an eagle, and fleet as a gazelle, and brave as a lion, to do the will of your Father who is in heaven..."
Pirkei Avot 5:20

Our Father

The term 'Our Father' in Hebrew 'Abinu' was a common phrase among Jewish people for addressing God. For in this phrase the character and nature of God towards his creation is summed up. For as a child looks to their earthly father as the provider, protector, comforter and the one who dispenses discipline, so also the ancients viewed God in a similar fashion. God was seen as the one who would provide for Israel, giving them their former and latter rains in due season to enable the crops to grow and flourish. He was the one who provided food for the first human couple in the Garden as well as manna and quail in the wilderness for Israel when they had just been freed from Egypt. He was the one who fed the hungry Prophet Elijah, by sending the ravens with food in their beaks and he was the one who sustained the nation of Israel in their land, a land flowing with milk and honey. As a good father would provide for his own children so God had provided for Israel, and not just Israel, but the whole human race. Jesus himself illustrates this truth about God perfectly,

"Which of you, if your son asks for bread, will give him a stone? Or if he asks for a fish, will give him a

snake? If you, then, though you are evil, know how to give good gifts to your children, how much more will your Father in heaven give good gifts to those who ask him!"

Jesus, Matthew Chapter 7:9-11

And like a good father, God is also a protector and a comforter of his children. Now, this isn't to say that bad things will never happen to good people, as we know this simply isn't true. But in ancient times God entered into a covenant with Israel 'as a nation' of people, to look after them and to provide for them. Today we call this covenant the Mosaic covenant. In this covenant (which is a fancy word for a legally binding agreement or promise), God promised to look after and protect Israel from the harm of invading nations, so long as they kept his covenant by obeying his Laws. And as long as Israel obeyed the Laws of the covenant, God would provide for them and protect them. However, when Israel began to chase after foreign gods and goddesses and despised their covenant with God, God's protection lifted and enemy nations invaded the land. Yet, God in his mercy sent them Prophet after Prophet to warn them of what was coming, to try and steer them back onto the path of blessing. He comforted them and encouraged them to remain true. But more often than not, Israel became stubborn and refused to listen to the messengers of God. It is difficult for us to understand today just how volatile and violent the ancient world was and what a magnificent blessing it was to have God's protection over a nation. God truly was and is a father to Israel and indeed the whole world.

In Heaven

Have you ever asked the question, 'Where was God before he created the Universe?' It is a fascinating question isn't it? Did he exist in another realm or dimension? Is this other realm or dimension uncreated like God, or was it created at a certain point in transcendent history? Does God need to dwell anywhere or is he just pure existence, from which all created spaces flow? And what is this ‘Heaven’ place that Jesus spoke so much about and where is it located? The questions are endless, but the Holy Bible does give us some insight into this fascinating world of ideas. To begin with, Jesus locates his Father in a place called Heaven, in Hebrew it is ‘HaShamayim’ or ‘the Heavens’. In Greek it is ‘Ouranos' which can mean ‘elevation, sky, or somewhere out there’. It points to a realm beyond this earthly existence and certain passages allude to the fact that this Heaven appears to be in a different space-time dimension to ours. It seems abundantly clear from Scripture that Heaven appears to be an immaterial reality and by that I mean that it is not composed of the same atomic stuff that our Universe is made from. Angels and the souls of the saved departed exist quite happily there without the need of a physical body. We have several instances in the

Scriptures of people ascending into Heaven, such as the account of the catching up of Elijah and the ascension of Jesus. One of the strangest accounts we read of is the reappearance of this same Elijah and Moses at the Transfiguration,

"After six days Jesus took with him Peter, James and John the brother of James, and led them up a high mountain by themselves. There he was transfigured before them. His face shone like the sun, and his clothes became as white as the light. Just then there appeared before them Moses and Elijah, talking with Jesus.

Peter said to Jesus, 'Lord, it is good for us to be here. If you wish, I will put up three shelters – one for you, one for Moses and one for Elijah.'

While he was still speaking, a bright cloud covered them, and a voice from the cloud said, 'This is my Son, whom I love; with him I am well pleased. Listen to him!'

When the disciples heard this, they fell face down to the ground, terrified. But Jesus came and touched them. 'Get up,' he said. 'Don't be afraid.' When they looked up, they saw no one except Jesus."

Matthew Chapter 17:1-8

Now it's one thing for an angel to come from Heaven, but for two human beings to reappear on earth is incredibly strange indeed. Where did they come from? How did they get there? Elijah had been caught up to heaven alive, Moses had travelled to heaven as a departed soul. But here they both are, seeming very much alive talking with Jesus and holding a conversation. And as quickly as they appear, they disappear back into a cloud of glory never to be seen again by the Apostles. Entrances into and exits from Heaven appear to be all around us. We just cannot see them and we are not the ones in control of them. It is the sacred, hallowed place where the Father dwells in unapproachable light.

When we study the Scriptures, I think the best we can do is to understand Heaven as the second abode of God, originally designed for his created angels and as a dwelling place for God to have a relationship with them. Prior to the creation of Heaven, I understand God to have existed in a perfect state, in and by himself as a loving trinity and that the sole existence was God himself. So questions such as, 'where did God exist?' or 'when did God exist?' become meaningless in relation to such a being. These terms refer to created places and not to God's eternal nature. From Scripture we can known that today, God has chosen to dwell in a self created realm called Heaven with his Holy Angels. And that in the future God himself will move from this Heaven to a third abode, the New Heaven and New Earth to dwell with us forever,

"Then I saw 'a new heaven and a new earth,' for the first heaven and the first earth had passed away, and there was no longer any sea. I saw the Holy City, the

new Jerusalem, coming down out of heaven from God, prepared as a bride beautifully dressed for her husband. And I heard a loud voice from the throne saying, 'Look! God's dwelling-place is now among the people, and he will dwell with them. They will be his people, and God himself will be with them and be their God. "He will wipe every tear from their eyes. There will be no more death" or mourning or crying or pain, for the old order of things has passed away."

Revelation Chapter 21:1-4

Hallowed Be Your Name

"All the members of the house of Israel are commanded to sanctify the great Name of God, as it is said "But I will be hallowed among the children of Israel" (Lev. 22:32). They are furthermore cautioned not to profane it, as it is said "Neither shall ye profane My holy Name" (Lev. 22:32)."

Mishnah Torah, Foundations of the Torah Chapter 5:1

Jewish people are so careful to hallow God's name, that many of them would rather call him 'HaShem' (The Name) than pronounce the name of God. The four lettered covenant name of God which we Translate YHWH, is referred to as the ineffable name, or the name that must never be spoken. And often when reading Jewish literature you will find the word God, spelt without the 'o' like this G-d. Therefore hallowing God's name is incredibly important to the Jewish people today, just as it was important to Jesus in the first century.

To hallow God's name means to keep it clean, pure and undefiled. A hallowed name is a holy name and we must use it in a proper way and with the greatest of respect.

"We will sanctify You & revere You, like the pleasant conversation, of the assembly of the holy Serafim (angels) that recite holiness thrice before You. And as it is written by Your prophet: And one calls to the

other & says : Holy, Holy, Holy is the L·rd of hosts; the entire world is filled with His glory. Those facing them, give praise & say: Blessed is the honor of the L·rd from His place. And in Your holy words it is written, stating: The L·rd will reign forever, your G·d, oh zion, for every generation, Halleluy·ah. (Praise G·d!)"

Weekday Shacharit, Amidah

Names are important, because names are attached to identities of individuals. If somebody 'gives you a bad name', it means that they have done or said something that puts your character in a negative light. In a similar way, when a follower of God commits an egregious error, God is often ridiculed for that person's mistake, because they bear his name. Under the Mosaic Law, the misuse of God's name could result in physical death. An example of this is the use of God's name when prophesying falsely,

"But a prophet who presumes to speak in my name anything I have not commanded, or a prophet who speaks in the name of other gods, is to be put to death.'
You may say to yourselves, 'How can we know when a message has not been spoken by the Lord?' If what a prophet proclaims in the name of the Lord does not take place or come true, that is a message the Lord has not spoken. That prophet has spoken presumptuously, so do not be alarmed."
Deuteronomy Chapter 18:20-22

God is so serious about his name being hallowed, that if someone were to say, 'Thus says the LORD…' when the LORD had not spoken, their life was to be forfeit. God's name is his badge of identity, and it is vitally important to God that people be able to trust in that name. For it is a reliable name because God's own identity and character stand behind it. When believers today use the expression 'OMG' or share a 'word' from the LORD, when it has not really originated with him, they do themselves a great harm without even realising it. As the LORD himself states,

"You shall not misuse the name of the Lord your God, for the Lord will not hold anyone guiltless who misuses his name."
Exodus Chapter 20:7

God's name is the holiest name in all of existence, because it is God's name. The Creator's name. The name of the King of the Universe. And when we use it, we must do so ever so carefully. When we pray and hallow God's name, we must do so reverently, tentatively, meditating upon his great nature and character. To hallow God's name is to sing pure praises from our heart to him and to live each day under the Sovereign umbrella of his rule. If we have at any time misused that holy and spotless name, then we need to repent immediately and ask God for his forgiveness. For as the Apostle John teaches,

"If we confess our sins, he is faithful and just and will forgive us our sins and purify us from all unrighteousness."

1 John Chapter 1:9

The hallowing of God's name in this Amidah of Jesus has one final aspect to it. An aspect that we will now investigate in the coming chapter, as Jesus cries out for his Father's Kingdom to come.

CHAPTER FIVE
The Kingdom Of The Boss

"Your kingdom come, your will be done, on earth as it is in heaven."

Jesus, Matthew Chapter 6:10

"Rabbi Yehoshua ben Korḥa said: Why, in the mitzva of the recitation of Shema, did the portion of Shema precede that of VeHaya im Shamoa? This is so that one will first accept upon himself the yoke of the kingdom of Heaven, the awareness of God and God's unity, and only then accept upon himself the yoke of the mitzvot..."

Mishnah Berakhot 2:2

The concept of a coming eternal Kingdom, where God's law (yoke) is obeyed and God's awareness or glory is seen, is rooted deeply within Judaism. The primary promise of this coming

Kingdom was given by God, through the Prophet Nathan to Kind David in these words,

"I declare to you that the Lord will build a house for you: when your days are over and you go to be with your ancestors, I will raise up your offspring to succeed you, one of your own sons, and I will establish his kingdom. He is the one who will build a house for me, and I will establish his throne for ever. I will be his father, and he will be my son. I will never take my love away from him, as I took it away from your predecessor. I will set him over my house and my kingdom for ever; his throne will be established for ever."'

Prophet Nathan, 1 Chronicles 17:10b-14

In these promises, also known as the Davidic covenant, David is promised seven specific things by God,

1. God himself will build a house for David

2. God will establish one of David's sons in his Kingdom
3. This coming son will build a house for God
4. His throne will be established forever
5. God will be his Father, and this descendant will be God's son
6. God will never remove his loving kindness from this son
7. This son will be set over God's house and Kingdom forever

So this coming son of David will be an everlasting King, ruling over an everlasting Kingdom. It is this unique son of David that will also be the son of God. Today we know this son of David to be the Lord Jesus Christ, the Messiah of Israel.

As previously mentioned, in Matthew Chapter 12, the offer given to Israel for the establishment of the Kingdom of God was withdrawn by Jesus. Up until this point, Jesus had freely offered the Kingdom through his teaching and miracle working ministry. However, when the leadership of Israel made the official decision that Jesus was not the Messiah (The King of the Kingdom), but rather a demon possessed madman, the Kingdom program shifted into the next stage of its three final forms. For the purpose of this discussion we will hereon call the three final forms as,

1. The Mystery Kingdom
2. The Millennial Kingdom
3. The Eternal Kingdom

As we understand the development of the Kingdom in these three forms, then we will understand why Jesus included this vital section in his Amidah prayer.

The First Form: The Mystery Kingdom

When the New Testament authors call something a mystery (Gk. mustērion) they are referring to a revelation that was not clearly taught or mentioned in the Old Testament Scriptures. An example of this can be found in 1 Corinthians 15, which pertains to the translation of Church saints,

"I declare to you, brothers and sisters, that flesh and blood cannot inherit the kingdom of God, nor does the perishable inherit the imperishable. Listen, I tell you a mystery: we will not all sleep, but we will all be changed – in a flash, in the twinkling of an eye, at the last trumpet. For the trumpet will sound, the dead will be raised imperishable, and we will be changed."

Apostle Paul, 1 Corinthians 15:50-52

In this case, Paul states that the revelation of the translation of Church saints into an imperishable body, is something that is not clearly mentioned in the Old Testament Scriptures. And try as hard as we might, we simply will not find this teaching there, even though this has always been a part of God's eternal plan. Another mystery also not clearly revealed is the current form of the Kingdom of God.

"He told them, 'The secret (Mystery) of the kingdom of God has been given to you. But to those on the outside everything is said in parables..."
Jesus, Mark 4:11

The Greek word translated here as secret is the same word for mystery (mustērion), and it is the mystery of the Kingdom that Jesus will now teach to his disciples, but to those who are not his disciples, the knowledge will be veiled in parables. The Mystery Kingdom then began at the official rejection of Jesus in Matthew Chapter 12 and will continue until the return, or Second coming of Jesus to establish the second form, the Millennial Kingdom.

To get a thorough understanding of the Mystery Kingdom one must study the parables to discover what Jesus taught about its development. Here I shall mention a brief sketch of an outline,

1. It will not appear as a physical Kingdom so that people can say, 'Here it is.'
2. It will begin very small like a mustard seed.
3. It will grow through the scattering of Gospel seed.
4. The King of the Kingdom will be absent throughout its duration.
5. It will grow to enormous proportions in the earth.
6. False teaching and demonic influence will spread throughout this Kingdom.
7. Both true and false converts will populate this Kingdom.
8. At the close of this Kingdom stage, the King will return and cast out of his Kingdom those who do not really belong in it.

So as we can see, this Kingdom will be a very imperfect one indeed. So now as we pray for God's Kingdom to come and his will to be done, we are looking further ahead to something greater than this current Mystery Kingdom.

The Second Form: The Millennial Kingdom

Now the Millennial Kingdom is not a mystery, for it is the primary focus of the Old Testament Scriptures. In fact the only new thing we learn about the Millennial Kingdom from New Testament revelation is its duration. Namely, it will last for exactly one thousand years. The Millennial Kingdom begins when Jesus returns from Heaven, and the transition occurs from the Mystery Kingdom to the Millennial Kingdom. During this time sin, sickness and death will be greatly reduced in the earth - although not entirely eradicated. To those of us who have already been transformed into immortal bodies, these three enemies will no longer pose a threat. But for those who came to a saving faith during the final days of the Tribulation period, they will enter the Kingdom in unregenerate bodies. Bodies still capable of conceiving and producing fallen human children, and hence why there is still a problem with sin, sickness and death in this form of the Kingdom. Isaiah rightly points this out,

"Never again will there be in it an infant who lives but a few days, or an old man who does not live out his years; the one who dies at a hundred will be thought a mere child; the one who fails to reach a hundred will be considered accursed. They will build houses and dwell in them; they will plant vineyards and eat their fruit. No longer will they build houses and others live in them, or plant and others eat. For as the days of a tree, so will be the days of my people; my chosen ones will long enjoy the work of their hands. They will not labour in vain, nor will they bear children doomed to misfortune; for they will be

a people blessed by the Lord, they and their descendants with them."

Isaiah 65: 20-23

The fact that Isaiah mentions people dying at a hundred during the Millennial Kingdom shows that these three last enemies have not been fully dealt with at this stage. Also when we look at the closing days of the Millennial Kingdom, we will once again see a massive uprising of wickedness in the earth,

"When the thousand years are over, Satan will be released from his prison and will go out to deceive the nations in the four corners of the earth – Gog and Magog – and to gather them for battle. In number they are like the sand on the seashore. They marched across the breadth of the earth and surrounded the camp of God's people, the city he loves. But fire came down from heaven and devoured them. And the devil, who deceived them, was thrown into the lake of burning sulphur, where the beast and the false

prophet had been thrown. They will be tormented day and night for ever and ever."

Apostle John, Revelation 20:7-10

So who could all of these wicked people be? They could not possibly be Israel, or the glorified Church saints. And you would be correct. They are in fact the children of those who came through the Tribulation into the Kingdom by the skin of their teeth. And even though Jesus is physically present on the earth, reigning in his glorified state, fallen humanity with their sin natures intact will still choose to rebel against him. So when we pray for God's Kingdom to come and for his will to be done, we are looking further ahead still to something greater than this future Millennial Kingdom. We are seeking the Father for his Eternal Kingdom.

The Third Form: The Eternal Kingdom

"Then I saw 'a new heaven and a new earth,' for the first heaven and the first earth had passed away, and there was no longer any sea. I saw the Holy City, the new Jerusalem, coming down out of heaven from God, prepared as a bride beautifully dressed for her husband. And I heard a loud voice from the throne saying, 'Look! God's dwelling-place is now among the people, and he will dwell with them. They will be his people, and God himself will be with them and be their God. "He will wipe every tear from their eyes. There will be no more death" or mourning or crying or pain, for the old order of things has passed away."

Apostle John, Revelation 21:1-4

And so now we come to the final form of the Kingdom of God. This is called the Eternal Kingdom, because as the name suggests it will be the permanent state of the Kingdom for all eternity. In this final form all sin, sickness and death will finally be done away with. There will be no more mourning, crying or pain, but a blissful existence in the presence of God. This Kingdom will be established on a new heaven and earth, or another universe. Albeit this universe will not be subject to sin and decay as this one is.

A brand new city of Jerusalem will also dwell upon this new earth and in appearance it will resemble a golden cube, 1,400 miles wide, high and long. Although the new universe may be inhabited by other stars and planets, heavenly luminaries will not be necessary for illumination upon the earth as the Apostle John continues,

"The city does not need the sun or the moon to shine on it, for the glory of God gives it light, and the Lamb is its lamp. The nations will walk by its light, and the kings of the earth will bring their splendour into it. On no day will its gates ever be shut, for there will be no night there."

Apostle John, Revelation 21:23-25

This final form of the Kingdom of God will be a glorious manifestation of God's divine will and pleasure. Those who dwell there will be fully regenerated and holy. It is in this final form that the Amidah prayer of Jesus will be fully realised.

So does this prayer only point to the final coming Kingdom in the new heaven and earth? Now, although the ultimate fulfilment will be realised at this future point in human history, that does not mean to say that we should not pray for God's will to be done here and now today. For when we pray this prayer, what we are really asking for is the saving of lost souls, to be brought under the authority and life of God. And so today as we pray to the Father, and ask for his will to be done on earth just as it is in heaven, let us keep in mind the hope of future glory, and the vital need of winning souls today.

CHAPTER SIX
The Bread Of The Boss

"Give us today our daily bread."
Jesus, Matthew Chapter 6:11

"Bless for us, L·rd, our G·d, this year, & all types of its produce for good, & provide dew & rain for blessing on the entire face of the land & quench the face of the earth, & satiate the entire world with Your good, & fill our hands from Your blessings & the wealth of the gifts of Your hands. Protect & save this year from any bad thing, & any kind of destruction, & any kind of retribution, & make for it good hope, & an ending of peace. Have compassion & mercy upon it & upon all of its produce & fruits, & bless it with rains of goodwill, blessing & benevolence, & let its end be with life, & satiety & peace, like the good years of blessing, for You are a good & benevolent

G·d & You bless the years. Blessed are You L·rd, Who blesses the years."

The Winter Weekday Shacharit, Amidah

In today's world of abundance, for many people, asking God for their daily provision of food seems like a waste of time. After all, most of us have a supermarket within driving distance, as well as a local convenience store within walking distance. So why on earth should we waste our time praying for something that is already right at our fingertips? However, thinking this way places too much confidence in humanity and dishonours the Lord who enables food to grow on the earth. Only in recent years, in the highly developed land in which I live, I have witnessed people fighting over clean water during a shortage, and others stocking up on cans of food, rice and toilet rolls. Things can change very quickly in society, so much so, that one minute we can behave like highly civilised people and in the next be clawing at one another for a can of baked beans. Now although this type of behaviour is rare, for we are still blessed by the Lord in this country, other countries around the world are not so blessed economically. It is a sad but true fact, that today millions of people around the world will starve of malnutrition whilst others will drink water which we would consider sewage. Not every person is as equally blessed as us, and this should cause us to give thanks to our kind and loving Heavenly Father, and think of how we can practically help those who are in need.

In Jesus' Amidah prayer he encourages us to pray not for bread, but for our daily bread, and this small additional word packs a powerful punch. One way to approach this small addition is to go back to the Scriptures that Jesus would have been familiar with in first century Israel. One type of literature was highly prized among the Jewish people, Wisdom literature,

"Two things I ask of you, Lord; do not refuse me before I die: keep falsehood and lies far from me; give me neither poverty nor riches, but give me only my daily bread. Otherwise, I may have too much and disown you and say, "Who is the Lord?" Or I may become poor and steal, and so dishonour the name of my God."

Proverbs 30: 7-9

The book of Proverbs was highly prized among the Jewish communities for its easily remembered sayings. Here we have the inspired utterance of Agur, son of Jakeh to Ithiel. In this utterance Agur asks the Lord for two things before he dies, namely that the Lord will keep deception from him and that the Lord would give him a modest lifestyle. In contrast with what many prosperity preachers spew these days, Agur recognises under inspiration that having too much provision can result in the danger of developing an arrogant and proud nature that opposes and rejects God's authority in one's life. And that the flip side of the coin, namely poverty, can cause a person to dishonour the name of God by living a life of crime to fill one's stomach. Therefore he asks the Lord to provide his daily food. Not too much and not too little, but just the right amount to keep him satisfied and in the place of humility and reliance upon the Lord.

As we think of the Lord Jesus' words here we are reminded of how the Lord provided for Israel when they took their first steps of freedom heading towards the promised land,

"Then the Lord said to Moses, 'I will rain down bread from heaven for you. The people are to go out each day and gather enough for that day. In this way I will test them and see whether they will follow my instructions. On the sixth day they are to prepare what they bring in, and that is to be twice as much as they gather on the other days."

Exodus 16: 4-5

The people of Israel were hungry and like all hungry people (including myself at times) they began to moan. They moaned against Moses and Aaron for delivering them from Egypt and they wished they had remained in Egypt sat around pots of food eating all they wanted. Apparently when you are hungry you quickly forget all of the horrors of forced labour! So the Lord spoke to Moses and said that he would rain down bread from heaven for the people. God instructed the people to go out each day and collect only the amount they needed for that specific day, it was to be their daily bread. If they collected too little they would go hungry, and if they collected too much it would rot. They needed only to collect their daily bread and rely upon the Lord each day to look after them. This was a trust exercise in which the people of Israel had to display their faith by putting it into practice and trusting in the promise of God, taking the Lord at his word. So each day they collected their daily bread, now of course some disobeyed out of a lack of faith or greed and they received what the Lord had warned. But the point of this whole experience should not be lost, to gather their daily bread was an act of trust and reliance upon the Lord. It was to have a childlike dependancy and reliance upon the Father. Jesus himself illustrates this point perfectly,

"So do not worry, saying, "What shall we eat?" or "What shall we drink?" or "What shall we wear?" For the pagans run after all these things, and your heavenly Father knows that you need them. But seek first his kingdom and his righteousness, and all these things will be given to you as well. Therefore do not worry about tomorrow, for tomorrow will worry about itself. Each day has enough trouble of its own."

Matthew 6:31-34

Here Jesus instructs his disciples not to act like the pagans do, that is in worrying about material possessions and chasing after riches. The Father in Heaven knows that we need these daily provisions for he created us to require them on a daily basis. Instead the disciples are to put God's will first, they are to seek God's Kingdom and God's righteousness and then the Father will take care of their daily needs. Again this is a step of faith on the disciples part, to see if they will come into a living relationship with the Father and to see if they will prioritise his Kingdom over their wants and desires here on earth. The importance of this life of faith is clearly echoed by Rabbi Eleazar,

"whoever has bread in his basket to eat today and says: What shall I eat tomorrow, meaning he does not know how he will acquire bread for tomorrow, he is nothing other than from those of little faith. One must trust in God to provide him with his sustenance."

Rabbi Eliezer Sotah 48b

And so we arrive full circle back to praying for and seeking the Kingdom of God. For it is in the Kingdom of God that the Lord's provision for his people will be fully realised. Firstly, as daily bread provided in the current Mystery Kingdom. Secondly, as a land flowing with milk and honey in the Millennial Kingdom, and finally as a bountiful paradise with new trees of life in the Eternal Kingdom - the Kingdom of God fully realised.

So in the Amidah prayer of Jesus, as his loyal disciples we must seek first his Kingdom program and then all of these other daily requirements will be added to us. This is just as much a test for us today as it was for the Israelites in their wilderness wanderings. Will we, like them, grumble over the fact that we are not keeping up with Joneses or will our attention and desires be differently focused? Will we continue to strive to have the best material possessions that money can buy, or will we use our resources to bring people into God's everlasting Kingdom? In a Church age that preaches so much on love and grace, will we be truly loving to our fellow man? Not in the giving of financial handouts and bacon butties, but in the sharing of the eternal Gospel that can save a soul from certain torment. Will we look to God to provide for us in our soul winning mission, or will we look to a manager for our next promotion and pay rise? For as disciples of the Lord Jesus Christ, we are all, each and every one of us, called to seek and save the lost. To advance God's Kingdom program, by inviting others into the great banquet of God's saving grace. So can we honestly restrain ourselves in asking, as Agur did, for the Lord not to give us too much? Can we honestly pray from the heart, 'give us today our daily bread?'

So this is the great challenge that lies before each of us who live here in this materialistic world. Are we capable of looking beyond our immediate concerns, worries and desires to catch a glimpse of the eternal future that awaits all mankind? Can we honestly say along with Job that,

"I have not departed from the commands of his lips; I have treasured the words of his mouth more than my daily bread."

Job 23:12

Maybe you are reading this right now and you are feeling a deep sense of conviction, so much so that you are tempted to put this book down and hide it under your coffee table. If so, I encourage you as a fellow traveller on this road of discipleship not to resist conviction but to yield to it, for conviction should not be confused with condemnation. The first encourages change in our lives whilst the second offers no hope of change. When we examine our hearts and we find in them all kinds of desires that we would rather cover up and pretend do not exist, we should instead confess them to the Father and ask for his life changing grace to do a work in us. This is how progress in the Christian life is made, sometimes in giant leaps, and at other times in gradual subtle steps. Only God can perform the miracle of changing a worldly, materialistic heart into a spiritual fountain of truth, love and grace that seeks to help others rather than ourselves. It is only by God's grace that we can genuinely pray the Amidah prayer of Jesus, in asking for a modest lifestyle that equips us and frees us to reach a world walking in the valley of the shadow of death. And it must be reached, for it is a sinful, fallen world and one in desperate need of God's forgiveness and redemptive power as we will discover in our next chapter together.

CHAPTER SEVEN
The Forgiveness Of The Boss

"And forgive us our debts, as we also have forgiven our debtors."

Jesus, Matthew Chapter 6:12

"Return us, our Father, to Your Torah & approach us, our King, to Your service, and bring us back to complete repentance before You. Blessed are You L·rd, Who desires repentance.
Pardon us, our Father, for we transgressed. Forgive us, our King for we sinned. For You are a good & forgiving G·d. Blessed are You L·rd, gracious One, Who abundantly pardons."

Weekday Shacharit, Amidah

Some years ago, in the backwoods of Kentucky a Sunday school teacher was finishing up her class by asking questions of her students. The final question posed was, "And what one thing must we do before we can receive forgiveness of our sin?" Turning to one another the pupils looked stumped until one little hand shot up into the air. And with a triumphant shout, little Connor McKreedy yelled, "Sin!"

Now although this was not quite the answer the Sunday School Teacher had been looking for, Connor was correct. Before any one of us can receive forgiveness of sin, we must first have sinned and being human beings with a fallen nature this does not come too hard to most of us. But what is sin? Sin can be described as missing the mark, or falling short of God's standards and it is something that all human beings do. Even if we were to look at just a couple of commandments from God's law such as 'you shall not lie' or 'you shall not steal' how many of us can truly say with confidence that we have never done either of these? And what about the greatest commandment, which calls us to love God with everything we have and to love our neighbour as we love ourselves? When we look into the perfect Law of God, it acts like a mirror that reflects back to us just how sinful we truly are as a race of people and just how powerless we are to try and obey God's law. There seems to be something on the inside of us, when it hears a command coming from the lips of God, that wants to automatically rebel against it. This is what we call the sin nature, which we have all inherited from our first parents in the Garden.

We are all in desperate need of forgiveness, yet for many of us we are too proud to ask God for it and so instead of approaching God humbly we run from God and hide behind our own creations of self righteousness often in the form of man crafted religious systems, works righteousness, meditation and kind acts. But none of these things will cleanse us of our sin or remove our guilt, for we must approach God on his basis and not on our own. We can choose to be obedient like Abel who approached God with a blood sacrifice as God required, or we can be like Cain who approached God with the works of his hands and fall short and sin further.

There is an old story of Robert the Bruce of Scotland, when he was leading his men in the fight against England for national independence. On one occasion the English had managed to acquire Bruce's own bloodhounds and set them upon Bruce's scent. As Bruce held out with a companion, they could hear the dogs howling in the distance as the English drew closer and closer. Bruce's companion cried out in terror, "We're done for, they have your scent!" To which Bruce replied, "Don't worry, it's going to be alright." And with that Bruce left his hiding place and headed towards the nearby river. As the hounds drew closer still, Bruce dived into the river scrubbing himself in the flowing waters before getting out the other side. A few moments later the bloodhounds arrived at the bank of the river sniffing and yelping, the scent had stopped there and they could no longer detect their master. The river had carried Bruce's scent away and a short time later Bruce was crowned King in Scotland.

Like Bruce we also have something chasing us down, and it is the justice of Almighty God. This justice can sniff out sin a mile off and requires that a blood sacrifice be made for it, life for life. And praise be to God, he has also provided a river for us, it is the river of his Son's own blood, the blood of the Lord Jesus Christ. When we repent (a word meaning to change our minds and turn back) and trust in the death, burial and physical resurrection of the Lord Jesus we can be cleansed by this flowing river and have the scent and stain of sin removed far from us. True forgiveness and acquittal can only be received through the atoning work of Jesus Christ on the cross and our placing of trust in this finished work. Now this is both a blessing, for there is nothing we have to do to earn forgiveness and salvation and a cursing for there is nothing we have to do to earn forgiveness and salvation. Why do I say this second part? It is because our sin nature wants to earn forgiveness, it wants to work for salvation and the last thing it wants to do is trust in the God it is running from. So this is why the grace of God is so important, for without it no-one could possibly be saved or forgiven. As the Apostle Paul rightly quotes,

"What shall we conclude then? Do we have any advantage? Not at all! For we have already made the charge that Jews and Gentiles alike are all under the power of sin. As it is written: 'There is no one righteous, not even one; there is no one who understands; there is no one who seeks God. All have turned away, they have together become worthless; there is no one who does good, not even one.'"
The Apostle Paul, Romans Chapter 3:9-12

Now, notice that phrase, 'there is no one who seeks God.' And this is why on another occasion the Lord Jesus Christ stated this,

"Yet there are some of you who do not believe.' For Jesus had known from the beginning which of them did not believe and who would betray him. He went on to say, 'This is why I told you that no one can come to me unless the Father has enabled them.'"

Jesus, John Chapter 6:64-65

So both this atoning sacrifice of Jesus and the enabling of the Father is required for us to be forgiven and saved from the demands of justice, we play no part in the saving of ourselves. We must simply ask the Father for forgiveness and trust he will do so, yet there is one requirement for this to be fully realised, we must also forgive those who have sinned against us.

I once heard the story of a Spanish father who had fallen out with his son. The son departed the family home and broke contact with his father and after the dust had settled, the father wanted to find his son and restore him to the family. After searching for months to no avail, he decided to place an advert in the Madrid newspaper, it read, “Dear Paco, if you’re reading this please meet me at the front of this newspaper office at 12 noon on Saturday. All is forgiven, I still love you, your Father.” On that Saturday more than eight hundred Paco’s turned up hoping it was their father reaching out to them. We all desperately want and need forgiveness, for we have all done some really stupid things which I am sure we all regret doing. There have been times in my own life when I have behaved or reacted in a certain way that I am ashamed of. It was a side of me that I didn’t realise existed and it is quite a shock to be confronted with a feeling, thought or behaviour coming from within, that you would rather did not exist. So this is why forgiveness is powerful and so crucial to the Kingdom of God program, for the Kingdom program seeks to eradicate sin in its entirety. In the current form, God seeks to cleanse our minds and consciences of sin. In the coming Millennial form, God seeks to cleanse our bodies of sin with resurrection power. And in the future Eternal form, God will eradicate all sin with the dissolving of this universe in fire and the creation of a new heaven and earth, perfected in every way.

A Three Stage Process

So forgiving others just as we have been forgiven is vitally important in promoting this Kingdom program. We must do everything in our power to restore broken down relationships through forgiveness. Now this is not to minimise what somebody may have done to you, forgiveness is not saying the offence did not happen, but rather it is acknowledging that the offence did occur, yet you want to restore things to how they used to be. Forgiveness is not cheap and it is not always easy, but it is something we must become good at, if we are to be Kingdom people. Forgiveness requires a three stage process,

Stage One: Confrontation. The offended person must approach the offender and point out the wrong doing.

Stage Two: The offender must apologise and put the offence right.

Stage Three: The offended person must forgive them on the basis of their repentance.

These three stages are brought out in Jesus' own teaching on forgiveness,

"If your brother or sister sins, go and point out their fault, just between the two of you. If they listen to you, you have won them over. But if they will not listen, take one or two others along, so that "every matter may be established by the testimony of two or three witnesses." If they still refuse to listen, tell it to the church; and if they refuse to listen even to the church, treat them as you would a pagan or a tax collector."

Jesus, Matthew 18:15-17

And also,

"If your brother or sister sins against you, rebuke them; and if they repent, forgive them. Even if they sin against you seven times in a day and seven times come back to you saying "I repent," you must forgive them."

Jesus, Luke 17:3

Forgiveness is so freeing to both parties involved. Holding on to unforgiveness does no harm to the offender, it only harms the health of the offended. How many people today suffer from chronic pain and health issues that lie rooted in an unforgiving heart? Bitterness is like an acid in your system that eats away at who you are both mentally and physically, and so forgiveness does not just help the offender, it also greatly benefits the offended. This is why forgiveness is such a big deal to Jesus and God, for they want a people who are one just as they are one.

My Nemesis

Some years ago, I worked in an insurance company. Now it was a pretty mundane job, and I was not much more than a data input clerk at the time. The only thing that made the job interesting was the people I worked with and the banter we would exchange. Then one day this all changed. A new person had arrived in our department, a man in his fifties that we will call Dennis. Now, Dennis was not the personable type, in fact he was downright rude and aggressive, and he took pleasure almost everyday mocking someone or speaking sharply and when he discovered that I was a follower of Jesus, boy did he let me have it! Day after day the abuse continued, yet day after day I continued to show him grace, for every mean word I would respond with a word of kindness and humour. This frustrated Dennis to the point that one day he stormed over to me shouting with his fists flailing, but I remained calm and just smiled. Every act of animosity was greeted with kindness and Dennis didn't know how to handle this. After several years of this, it was time for me to move on and find another job, and so on that final day in the office I decided to buy Dennis a goodbye present. I purchased a huge box of chocolates along with a goodbye card and in it I wrote,

"Goodbye Dennis, thank you for all of your help and kindness. I am going to miss you most of all. Your friend, Paul."

And with that I left the present on his desk and looking around the office one final time, I departed from that company. Some weeks later, I bumped into an old friend who also worked with Dennis, and they related what happened when he turned up to work the following day. Grabbing the gift and unwrapping it, and then looking at my message in the card, he burst into tears and broke down in front of everyone in the office. That is the power of love, that is the power of forgiveness.

The Amidah prayer of Jesus encourages each one of us to seek restoration with God and with our fellow man, for this is the ideal of the coming Kingdom of God. When we pray this prayer and when we act upon this, we are allowing God's will to be done on earth, just as it is done in heaven. For we have an enemy, a malevolent being who opposes the will of God and seeks to disrupt the Kingdom influence in this earth and we will be discussing his tactics in our next chapter.

CHAPTER EIGHT
The Protection Of The Boss

"And lead us not into temptation, but deliver us from the evil one, for yours is the kingdom and the power and the glory forever. Amen."

Jesus, Matthew Chapter 6:13

"Behold, please, our affliction & fight our battle, & speedily redeem us, [with] a complete redemption, for Your Name. For You G·d, are a mighty Redeemer, Blessed are You L·rd, Redeemer of Yisrael.
Heal us, L·rd, & we will be healed. Save us & we will be saved, for You are our Praise. And bring a cure & healing for all of our ailments, & all our pains, & all our wounds for, G·d You are a compassionate & faithful healer. Blessed are You L·rd, Who heals the ill of His people, Yisrael."

Weekday Shacharit, Amidah

As Jesus now begins to conclude his summation of the Jewish Amidah prayer, he does so with a plea to God asking for righteous guidance and protection from evil. This is an incredibly important prayer for each and every one of us, because in this age we have three very strong enemies to contend with,

1. The flesh
2. Satan
3. The world

Our first enemy is the flesh, which is this fallen body into which we have been born with all of its chemical desires wanting to be fulfilled. It is a body that has inherited the sin nature from our first parents and it has the innate desire to rebel against the commands of God. So, for instance, when the command of God comes which states, "You shall not lie." The sin nature within our flesh immediately springs to life and urges us to lie.

Our second enemy is Satan, a fallen Cherub who seeks to destroy God's creation in the earth. He is the originator of sin and it was he who deceived our first mother Eve, to rebel against God in taking the forbidden fruit of the tree of the knowledge of good and evil. Satan, of course is not alone in his diabolical plan to destroy God's image in humanity, for he is assisted in this battle by numerous other fallen angels who seek to do his bidding.

Our third and final enemy is the world itself, a fallen place with a system of government and commerce that is less than desirable for a true follower of the Lord Jesus Christ. It is a system that seeks to stamp out God's authority in the world, whilst all the time appealing to the carnal needs and wants of the flesh.

And all three would love nothing more than for you and me to indulge in sin, ruining ourselves and our relationship with God. The real danger of course lies in the fact that sin is so pleasurable, and if it were not we simply would not indulge in it. After all, how many of us are tempted to go on a diet, get some exercise, or fill out a tax return form before the necessary deadline? How many of us are tempted to clean out the sink, eat foods we detest and walk around in the freezing cold wearing only a pair of shorts? These temptations never come our way (unless we are incredibly strange) because the fulfilment of these temptations would never bring us pleasure, and as the human race we are always trying to avoid pain and gain more pleasure. This pleasure driven temptation is perfectly illustrated in the story of two very large sisters called Mavis and Betty.

Mavis and Betty's Undoing

Mavis and Betty were sisters, two very large sisters who used to live together in a small thatched cottage in the Cotswolds. Mavis and Betty loved nothing more than to eat, and their favourite tasty treat was homemade cream cake. Now Mavis and Betty were dab hands in the kitchen, so each day early in the morning, they would mix up their ingredients and bake a delicious cake. Once it had come out of the oven they would fill it with fresh cream and cover it in frosted icing. When time came for their afternoon tea, they would bring the cake out on a trolley, and cutting thin slice after thin slice they would devour the whole thing between them. One day however this did not go to plan. As Mavis leaned forward to cut the cake, she realised that she had become wedged in her armchair, unable to move. Betty also had grown rather rotund and after a wiggle here and a waggle there she managed to free herself from her seat.

"What are we going to do?" asked Mavis, "We can't carry on eating like this, we will never get out of our front door if we do not stop now!"

Betty agreed and came up with a plan, "This will be the last cake we ever bake. But as it would be a shame to throw this beautiful cake away, let us put it in a box and have just a little nibble everyday."

"Oh no!" replied Mavis, "That would be too tempting for me. How about we tie some ribbon around the box to stop us getting in?"

"That would never work," replied Betty, "all we would need to do is cut the ribbon with a pair of scissors. Instead, why don't we lock the cake away in the cupboard?"

"But then we could unlock the cupboard and eat the cake, the temptation would be too strong." Replied Mavis. "Instead why don't you get a ladder and place the cake on top of the roof, out of sight and out of mind?"

"Oh but on a windy day like today, the smell of the cake would waft down the chimney and this would be far too tempting." Insisted Betty, "How about we just eat this one, right now, and never bake another cake again?"

"Hmmm… Agreed!' replied Mavis.

And that's just what the sisters did, they ate that cake there and then, cream and all, until not a single crumb of cake could be seen or sniffed. On the following day they agreed between themselves never to eat another cream cake again… that is, after the fresh one they had just baked that morning.

The Three Seats of Power

That is the problem of sin, it is too tempting and without God's help and grace operating in our lives we will always succumb to its power. Just like Edmond succumbed to the power of the White Witch when tempted with Turkish Delight in C.S. Lewis's, Chronicles of Narnia. We read in the Gospels that Jesus was led into the wilderness to be tested by Satan, this was in order to prove his power over the three seats of power, lust of the flesh, the lust of the eyes and the pride of life, in order to establish his rightful Messianic position in Israel. It is in these same three areas that believers like you and me will be tested, as the Apostle John confirms,

"Do not love the world or anything in the world. If anyone loves the world, love for the Father is not in them. For everything in the world – the lust of the flesh, the lust of the eyes, and the pride of life – comes not from the Father but from the world. The world and its desires pass away, but whoever does the will of God lives for ever."

Apostle John, 1 John 2:15-17

The lust of the flesh refers to those temptations that are felt within. The lust of the eyes refers to those temptations that are seen. The pride of life refers to those temptations where we place self importance over and in place of the authority of God.

But unlike Jesus who proved himself able to overcome these three areas of temptation, the Israelites under Moses, succumbed in their forty year wilderness wanderings. In fact the entire history of the Jewish people is one marked by rebellion against their Creator in these three areas. A history that they are all too familiar with and which is reflected in their prayer for blessing,

"May it be Your will, O Lord my God, that You make me lie down in peace and give me my portion in Your Torah, accustom me to mitzvot and do not accustom me to transgression, lead me not into error, nor into iniquity, nor into temptation nor into disgrace. May the good inclination have dominion over me and may the evil inclination not have dominion over me. Save me from an evil mishap and evil diseases."

Prayer for Blessing, Berakhot 60b

The Jewish people understood human nature to have two inclinations or drives that were in opposition with each other. The good inclination that sought to do the will of God and the evil inclination that sought to rebel against God. And for the Jew, it was a constant struggle to war against the evil inclination in order to do the will of God. The Apostle Paul confirms this struggle in the book of Romans,

"I do not understand what I do. For what I want to do I do not do, but what I hate I do. And if I do what I do not want to do, I agree that the law is good. As it is, it is no longer I myself who do it, but it is sin living in me. For I know that good itself does not dwell in me, that is, in my sinful nature. For I have the desire to do what is good, but I cannot carry it out. For I do not do the good I want to do, but the evil I do not want to do – this I keep on doing. Now if I do what I do not want to do, it is no longer I who do it, but it is sin living in me that does it.

So I find this law at work: although I want to do good, evil is right there with me. For in my inner being I delight in God's law; but I see another law at work in me, waging war against the law of my mind and making me a prisoner of the law of sin at work within me. What a wretched man I am! Who will rescue me from this body that is subject to death? Thanks be to God, who delivers me through Jesus Christ our Lord!"

The Apostle Paul, Romans 7:15-25

Paul here is describing the life of the Jew who does not have Christ living in them. It is a struggle between the image of God within and the inherited sin nature from Adam and Eve. In our minds and consciences we know the good we ought to do, for we still bear the image of God, marred though it has become, but the sin nature is often too strong and our will often succumbs to it. With the addition of God's Law given to the Jewish people, the sin nature within has more to rebel against. Thus showing just how truly sinful as a race we have become. Paul laments over this position, but then offers hope in his concluding remarks, for it is Jesus Christ who can deliver us from this body that is subject to death. Christ's grace and power are more than enough to enable you and me to overcome all of the temptations of the enemy and to keep us safe from the harm that he would want to inflict upon us.

This is often why the enemy tries so hard to pull us away from our prayer and study time with God, because it is during this time that we get re-energised to serve him. It is during these moments that our conscience becomes renewed and highly sensitised to sin and further grace is given to resist and overcome our three enemies of the Flesh, Satan and the World. And if we have sinned against God then we must remember that old and certain promise that,

"If we confess our sins, he is faithful and just and will forgive us our sins and purify us from all unrighteousness."

The Apostle John, 1John 1:9

Notice what it says here, not just that God will forgive us of our sins, but that he will purify us from all unrighteousness. This is grace power at work within us, to change us and conform us to his will to the glory of Jesus Christ alone. You see with God's help it is possible to live a pure life, and a pure second can turn into a pure minute, and a pure minute can turn into a pure hour, and a pure hour can turn into a pure day. With God holiness is a real possibility, without God holiness is an unattainable carrot dangling on a stick in front of a hungry donkey.

The Amidah Conclusion

And so we come to the conclusion of the Amidah prayer of Christ, where Matthew adds the doxology adapted from King David in 1 Chronicles,

"Yours, Lord, is the greatness and the power and the glory and the majesty and the splendour, for everything in heaven and earth is yours.

Yours, Lord, is the kingdom; you are exalted as head over all."

King David, 1Chronicles 29:11

For in conclusion, the whole Amidah prayer of Jesus is focused upon one thing, the coming ultimate fulfilment of the Kingdom of God. A future age when God's will is fully realised among his own people. An age when true prosperity will overflow and the enemies of God will have been vanquished. An age where this perfected reality will roll over into eternity. Jesus, as we all should be, was focused on the end goal of his life's mission which was to destroy the forces of evil and to bring as many people into the rule and reign of God as would freely choose to accept him. And so if we are to Pray like the Boss, then we must pray with this future fulfilment of the Kingdom program in mind and live each day to bring about its arrival.

Closing Remarks

Dear reader, God loves you. And he delights in having a daily relationship with you, so much so that he had decided before the world began to send his only begotten Son into this world to die as an atoning sacrifice for all of our sins, past, present and future. He loves us so much that he decided to base our forgiveness and salvation on the one thing that all relationships are founded upon and that is trust. Today he is asking us to trust him with our eternal souls, to place our faith in him and in the fact that he is able to forgive us entirely and to redeem us from the way of life that leads to death. The evidence in which we can place our trust is the resurrection of the Lord Jesus Christ from the dead, for if God has the power to resurrect Jesus, then he has the power to resurrect you and I. So can I encourage you now, if you have not already done so, to trust in God, and to place your faith in the atoning work of Jesus, which was carried out upon that old rugged cross in

Jerusalem almost two thousand years ago. And if you have already trusted in this remarkable work of God, to tell others about it too. For it would not be right for us to own a ticket to eternal life, to then ignore the blight of our neighbours, friends and family. As members of the mystery Kingdom, we are each called in like manner to our Saviour's service, to the work of winning souls for the Father. For in this is the whole purpose of life, to obey God and to love others.

"For God so loved the world that he gave his one and only Son, that whoever believes in him shall not perish but have eternal life. For God did not send his Son into the world to condemn the world, but to save the world through him. Whoever believes in him is not condemned, but whoever does not believe stands condemned already because they have not believed in the name of God's one and only Son."

Jesus Christ, John 3:16-18

APPENDIX
The Jewish Amidah Prayer

1. The God of History

Blessed are You Lord, our God, and God of our fathers, God of Abraham, God of Isaac and God of Jacob. The great, the mighty and the awesome God. Exalted God. Who bestows good kindness. He possesses everything and recalls the kindness of the patriarchs. And brings the redeemer to their children's children, for His Name's sake, with love. King, helper, saviour and a shield, blessed are You Lord, Shield of Abraham.

2. The God of Nature

You are mighty forever, my Lord, You revive the dead - Greatly capable of saving. You sustain the living with loving-kindness. You revive the dead with great compassion. You support the fallen and heal the ill. And You release those bound. And You fulfil Your faithfulness to those who sleep in the ground. Who is like You, Master of [all] powers, King, Who causes death and gives life and causes salvation to sprout. And You are trustworthy to revive the dead. Blessed are You Lord, Who revives the dead.

3. Sanctification of God

We will sanctify You and revere You, like the pleasant conversation, of the assembly of the holy Seraphim (six winged angels) that recite holiness thrice before You. And as it is written by Your prophet: And one calls to the other and says : Holy, Holy, Holy is the Lord of hosts; the entire world is filled with His glory. Those facing them, give praise and say: Blessed is the honour of the Lord from His place. And in Your holy words it is written, stating: The Lord will reign forever, your God, oh Zion, for every generation, Hallelujah. (Praise God!)

You are Holy, and Your Name is holy, and Your holy ones will praise You every day, forever. Blessed are You Lord the Holy God.

4. Prayer for Understanding

You graciously bestow knowledge to man, and teach mortals understanding, graciously bestow upon us from Yourself wisdom, understanding and knowledge. Blessed are You Lord, Who graciously bestows knowledge.

5. For Repentance

Return us, our Father, to Your Torah and approach us, our King, to Your service, and bring us back to complete repentance before You. Blessed are You Lord, Who desires repentance.

6. For Forgiveness

Pardon us, our Father, for we transgressed. Forgive us, our King for we sinned. For You are a good and forgiving God. Blessed are You Lord, gracious One, Who abundantly pardons.

7. For Deliverance

Behold, please, our affliction and fight our battle, and speedily redeem us, [with] a complete redemption, for Your Name. For You God, are a mighty Redeemer, Blessed are You Lord, Redeemer of Israel.

8. For Healing

Heal us, Lord, and we will be healed. Save us and we will be saved, for You are our Praise. And bring a cure and healing for all of our ailments, and all our pains, and all our wounds for, God You are a compassionate and faithful healer. Blessed are You Lord, Who heals the ill of His people, Israel.

9. For Needs

[In Summer]

Bless us, Lord, our God, in all the works of our hands and bless our years with dews of favour, blessing and benevolence, and let its end be with life, and satiety and peace, like the best years of blessing, for You are a good and benevolent God and You bless the years. Blessed are You Lord, Who blesses the years.

[In Winter]

Bless for us, Lord, our God, this year, and all types of its produce for good, and provide dew and rain for blessing on the entire face of the land and quench the face of the earth, and satiate the entire world with Your good, and fill our hands from Your blessings and the wealth of the gifts of Your hands. Protect and save this year from any bad thing, and any kind of destruction, and any kind of retribution, and make for it good hope, and an ending of peace. Have compassion and mercy upon it and upon all of its produce and fruits, and bless it with rains of goodwill, blessing and benevolence, and let its end be with life, and satiety and peace, like the good years of blessing, for You are a good and benevolent God and

You bless the years. Blessed are You Lord, Who blesses the years.

10. For Gathering of the Exiles

Sound a great Shofar (rams horn for Messiah), for our freedom, and raise a flag to gather our exiles, and assemble us together quickly from the four corners of the earth to our land (of Israel). Blessed are You, that assembles the displaced of His people, Israel.

11. For the Righteousness of God

Restore our Judges (of the Sanhedrin) as at first, and our advisers as in the beginning, and remove from us sorrow and groan, and rule upon us speedily, You alone Lord, with lovingkindness and compassion, with righteousness and justice Blessed are You, Lord, King Who loves righteousness and justice.

12. For the Destruction of Apostates (added later)

For the informers and the heretics, let there be no hope. And all the wicked, let them perish in an instant, And all Your enemies and all Your haters, may they quickly be terminated, and as for a wicked government, may You uproot and smash and terminate and subdue them speedily in our days. Blessed are You, Lord, Who smashes the enemies and subdues wicked. (the Heretics)

13. For the Righteous

Upon the righteous and the pious, and all the remnant of Your people, the House of Israel, and on their elders, and on the remnant of the academies of [Torah] sages, and upon the righteous converts and upon us, awaken, please, Your mercy Lord, our God, and give us good reward, to all that have true faith in Your Name, and place our lot with them, and upon Your great mercy, we truly rely. Blessed are You, Lord, a support and an assurance, for the righteous.

14. For the Rebuilding of Jerusalem

Dwell within Jerusalem Your city, as You spoke about, and the throne of David, Your servant, speedily prepare it within it, and build it an eternal structure speedily in our days. Blessed are You, Lord, Who builds Jerusalem.

15. For the Messiah

The offspring of [the Kingship of] David, Your servant, may you speedily cause to blossom, and raise his horn (i.e., Power) with Your salvation, for Your salvation, for we hope for and look forward to all day. Blessed are You, Lord, Who causes the horn of salvation to sprout.

16. For the Answering of Prayer

Hear our voice Lord our God, merciful Father, have pity and mercy upon us, and accept with mercy and favour our prayers, for You are God, Who hears prayers and supplications. And from before You, our King, do not send us back empty [handed], grace us [with benevolence]. Blessed are You, our God, Who hears prayer.

17. For the Restoration of Temple Service

Find favour, Lord, our God, in Your people Israel, and to their prayers turn, and restore the [divine offering] service to the inner Sanctuary of Your house, and the fires [of the offerings] of Israel and their prayers speedily lovingly accept with favour, and let You continually have satisfaction from the service of Your people Israel. And may our eyes see Your return to Zion with compassion. Bless You, Lord, Who returns His Divine Presence to Zion.

18. Thanksgiving for God's Unfailing Mercies

We are grateful to You, that You are He Who is the Lord, our God, and God of our fathers forever, and our Rock, the Rock of our lives and You are He Who is a Shield of salvation. For each and every generation, we will thank You and will relate Your praise, upon our lives that are placed in Your Hands, and upon our souls, that are entrusted in Your hands (when we sleep), and upon Your miracles that all day are with us, and all Your wonders and goodness at all times, at night, and morning and afternoon. The Good [One], for Your mercy never ends, The Merciful [One are You], for Your loving-kindness never ceases, forever we have hope in You.

19. For Peace

Establish peace, good, and blessing, life, grace and kindness, and compassion upon us and upon all Israel, Your Nation, and bless us our Father all of us together with the light of Your countenance, For with the light of Your countenance, You gave us, Lord, our God, Torah and Life, Love and Kindness, Righteousness and Compassion, Blessing and Peace, and it is Good in Your eyes to bless us, and to bless all Your people Israel, with great force and peace. Blessed are You Lord, Who Blesses His people of Israel with Peace. Amen.

Stay In Touch!

If you enjoyed this book please be sure to tell others about it.

For further resources sign up and subscribe to our social media channels:

FACEBOOK
Compelling Reason

YOUTUBE
Reasonable Faith UK - Compelling Reason

Thank you for all of your kind support and prayers.
Your friend and servant,

Paul Lyndon Burtwell.

Printed in Great Britain
by Amazon

60446110R00077